Photographs by Horatio Ross, 1801–1886

Yale Center for British Art
New Haven, Connecticut

Published on the occasion of an exhibition
at the Yale Center for British Art
September 14 – November 28, 1993

Library of Congress Catalogue Card Number 93-060991
ISBN 0-930606-70-1

Designed by Julie Lavorgna
Photography by Richard Caspole
Prepared for press by GIST Inc.
Printed by Van Dyck Columbia

Front cover: cat. 33, [Waterfall]

Back cover: Justine Henriette Ross
The Photographer in His Studio, c. 1858
Collection of the J. Paul Getty Museum
Malibu, California

Foreword

Last autumn the Yale Center for British Art presented *Victorian Landscape Watercolors*. While that exhibition was in preparation, the album of photographs that forms the heart of this show was brought to my attention. I was immediately struck by the parallels between the watercolors and the contemporary works of this Scottish amateur photographer. With the Victorian watercolorists, I was concerned with the push and pull of tradition against new approaches to nature. This same dynamic is also to be found in Horatio Ross's photographs, as Chris Titterington so persuasively argues in the following essay.

While the Yale Center does not as yet have a photographic collection of its own, it has long been clear to us that our institution could not adequately represent British art of the last century and a half if we ignored photography. *Photographs by Horatio Ross, 1801–1886* thus takes its place in an ongoing series of loan exhibitions exploring the work of British photographers.

We thank Janet Lehr for suggesting an exhibition on Ross, for enthusiastically championing this underappreciated figure, and for supplying most of the photographs in the show. For the loan of Ross's daguerreotypes, we are indebted to the Collection of Prints, Drawings, and Paintings of the Victoria and Albert Museum, London. Special thanks go to Chris Titterington, Assistant Curator of Photographs there, for his assistance as well as his splendid essay. He would like to express his gratitude to Hans P. Kraus, Jr., Mark Haworth-Booth, Richard Ormond, Sara Stevenson, Richard Ovenden, Carolyn Bloore, Nick Norman, Walter Jackson Bate, and especially to Sue Percival. Finally, I would like to acknowledge the invaluable contributions of colleagues at the Yale Center, especially Barbara Allen, José Branco, Richard Caspole, Chick Cerillo, Constance Clement, Theresa Fairbanks, Christopher Foster, Timothy Goodhue, Marilyn Hunt, Richard Johnson, Julie Lavorgna, Patrick Noon, and Lorelei Watson.

Scott Wilcox
Associate Curator for Prints and Drawings

Horatio Ross: Photography and the Picturesque
by Chris Titterington

It seems obvious, in retrospect, that nineteenth-century photographers should share the aesthetic concerns of their contemporaries working within painting—that they should, in other words, be firmly embedded within their own time. We should not, then, be surprised to discover photographs from the 1850s that have much in common with watercolors by David Cox, George Fennel Robson, William Turner of Oxford or, indeed, the oils of Edwin Landseer. The major histories of photography, however, have been relatively oblivious to this truth: as the products of modernist historical method, they have exhibited a preoccupation with a linear development within a single medium. Recent scholarship has attempted to correct this state of affairs, and it is thus highly appropriate that this exhibition should take place within the context of the collection of oils and watercolors at the Yale Center for British Art.

Horatio Ross is particularly interesting in respect of this shared aesthetic, for his photographs display not only a high degree of pictorial sophistication but a pressing ambition for the new medium. Indeed, as far as iconography is concerned, his work would not have looked significantly out of place at the annual exhibitions of the Society of Painters in Water Colours during the 1850s. I say "significantly" less from the point of view of the strict optical naturalism inherent to his medium than from the point of view of his aesthetic. (The Society had, after all, hung many works of a similarly rigorous empiricism by Cornelius Varley since as far back as 1804.)[1] Aesthetically Ross owes allegiance to a slightly older generation—to those artists born in the 1770s or 1780s and schooled in the Sublime and the high Picturesque of the late eighteenth century—figures such as David Cox, who were coming to the end of their careers during the period of Ross's most creative activity in the 1850s.

In respect of his aesthetic ambitions for his photography, Ross is fairly representative of the culture of wealthy gentlemen amateurs to which he himself belonged and through whom the main history of photography before 1860 can be traced. It has often been remarked that during the 1860s the aesthetic content of photography declined or at least veered away from the fine art values that it had carried in the previous two decades. In some measure this must represent a shift in the economic and social class of its main practitioners and consumers, for the main figures of the 1840s and 1850s had been schooled in the classics and educated visually towards a certain canon of taste. Indeed, they belonged to an elite which had access to lessons in watercolor from some of the established names of the period. In fact, it is possible to trace direct points of connection between the two media through figures such as the Delamottes or the Varleys—William Delamotte being a founding member of the Society of Painters in Water Colours and his son Phillip going on to become photographer to the Royal Family,[2] while the sons of Cornelius Varley became photographers, and he himself was a lens maker.

If the practitioners of the new medium were anxious to demonstrate its potential as a vehicle for art and were thus committed to establishing it within the accepted aesthetic canon, their efforts were not altogether appreciated from within that canon. For the indexical or automatic, mechanical quality inherent to photography seemed to many to run counter to the accepted norms of skill and "touch" that were the ultimate guarantors of human artifice. Put like that and using the term "artifice," one can see that photography's indexical quality is part of the broad cult of the natural; in fact, for many observers from outside the medium, photography seemed altogether too natural and was not, indeed, artificial enough. One of the inventors of photography, William Henry Fox Talbot, for instance, had named his early publication of examples of photography *The Pencil of Nature*. For some this implied too radical an exclusion of human sensibility and consciousness. In this there is something of a paradox, or at least a contradiction, for in this aspect of its nature, photography was actually profoundly congruent with the main thrust of theory that underpins the dominant aesthetic of the day. Indeed, it is clear that the very birth of the medium was conditioned by the anti-rationalism that informed the theoretical environment of the late eighteenth and early nineteenth century.

Horatio Ross was born in 1801, the only son of Hercules Ross of Rossie Castle near Montrose. The family was wealthy and might accurately be described as having recently become part of the elite of Scottish landed gentry. His grandfather had been an excise officer at Glasgow, and his father, though we do not at present know how, appears to have made his fortune in Jamaica during the 1760s. It was there that he had met and become friends with Horatio, later Lord, Nelson for whom Horatio Ross was named. (Nelson was, in fact, his godfather.) In 1805 Hercules built Rossie Castle on his estate. The details of Horatio's life (beyond his sporting fame) are at present sketchy. His education is, for example, unknown; however, we do know that at eighteen he joined the army, serving in the 14th Light Dragoons until 1826 when he retired with the rank of Captain. In 1831 he was returned for Parliament as member for the Aberdeen boroughs and later sat until 1834 as member for Montrose. He lived at Rossie until 1853 when he sold it and moved to Netherley in Kincardineshire. His contemporary reputation rested on his sporting abilities as an athlete, a rider, and marksman, either on the range or the moor. This reputation amounted to a national celebrity that lingered on long after his death. In order to give a flavor of this, I will quote extensively from his entry in the 1906 *Dictionary of National Biography:*

> Between 1825 and 1830 Captain Ross was a conspicuous figure in the world of sport, making and winning many matches for large sums in shooting and steeplechasing. With his best steeplechaser, Clinker...he beat Lord Kennedy's Radical in a match for £1000 a side in March 1826, riding himself; this match is said to have been the first steeplechase held in this country.... Ross also won a sculling match over the seven miles course between Vauxhall Bridge and Hammersmith. On another occasion he walked without stopping from the river Dee to Inverness, a distance of ninety-seven miles.
>
> One of the most remarkable of Captain Ross's shooting exploits was his match with Colonel (afterwards General) George Anson, on 1 Nov. 1828, for £1000 a side. They were to shoot partridges against each other...starting at sunrise and finishing at sunset. About a quarter of an hour from the finish Osbaldeston rode over and told Ross that his opponent was dead beat...and proposed to draw stakes. Anson was then one bird ahead, but could go no further. Ross, reflecting that killing two birds in ten minutes was hardly a chance on which to risk £1000, accepted.... Anson then had to be lifted into his carriage, while Ross offered to walk any one present to London for £500.
>
> For nearly thirty years Ross led the life of a quiet Scottish laird, when suddenly the volunteer movement and the consequent development of rifle-shooting in 1859 brought him again conspicuously before the world... in 1862 the international match for the Elcho shield was instituted.... Captain Ross then, and for ten years afterwards, acted as the Scottish Captain.... [In 1867] he won the cup of the Cambridge Long Range Rifle Club against nearly all the best shots of the three kingdoms. The competition extended up to eleven hundred yards, a test of nerve, judgement, and, most of all, eyesight, which it would seem wholly impossible for any man in his sixty-sixth year to stand successfully.

His obituary in the *Scotsman* on the 7th of December 1886 states that "as a deer-stalker he had no equal.... during the long period of seventy years he never missed a season." He was said to have killed seventy-five deer in the 1837 season and on one occasion in the forest of Mar to have killed thirteen deer with fourteen shots; on another occasion he is recorded as having killed eight stags in ten minutes. A number of portraits of him are known, among them several oils by the great sports painter Landseer, a daguerreotype self portrait (cat. 1), a full-length portrait of him with his camera by his wife (back cover), and several photographs by Roger Fenton of him and his sons at shooting matches in the 1860s.[3]

His recent reputation, of course, rests entirely on his photographic activities. A contemporary account suggests that he became involved in photography in 1840, just one year after the announcement of its invention; however, no examples have survived until those of 1847: a group of daguerreotypes attributed to him in the Victoria and Albert Museum, London (cat. 1–7). In 1849 he is known to have taken lessons in the calotype process from James Ross (no relation) in Edinburgh, and in 1856 he was one of the founding members of the Photographic Society of Scotland (indeed, he appears to have been the prime mover), becoming vice president in 1857 and president in 1858. In the later 1850s he took up the new collodion process (see Glossary). The bulk of the photographs known by him appear to be from this period, possibly extending into the late 1860s. Most of the photographs in the present exhibition originate from the album of 110 albumen prints of circa 1858–68 that he presented to his wife, Justine H. Ross, in 1870.[4]

I have made claims for Ross's aesthetic ambition, and I think that on the most basic level we can see this in the sheer scale of his pictures. Both the calotype and collodion processes at this date (before enlargement was in general use) involved the use of large-scale negatives, which were then contact printed to form the final image. The dimensions of the pictures in question here all approach twelve inches by fourteen. The gigantic camera this required can be seen in Mrs. Ross's portrait of Horatio preparing a negative. Here I should make clear that the context of modern photography gives a false idea of the weight of intention attached to a nineteenth-century photograph. We tend, anachronistically, to suppose that the conveniences of the modern camera and the small rolls of manufactured film that it uses attach also to the earlier period. It is particularly dangerous when looking at what appear to be casual or insignificant images to fall under this misapprehension. Images produced during the 1850s involved a great deal of labor. Thus, seemingly insignificant subjects may accrue an even greater interest than those depicting obviously important things. Ross himself is eloquent on the difficulties of his art, and at a meeting of the Photographic Society of Scotland in 1857 he made the following observations:

> It may amuse the meeting if I describe my arrangements for conveying my apparatus over some of the wildest scenes in the Highlands, and taking views many miles distant from my house.
>
> I had to take to the spot where I had intended to operate no less than 15 articles, of which the want of any one would have been fatal. I may as well enumerate them: 1. A [dark] tent. 2. The Camera. 3. The lens. 4. The legs for the camera. 5. The glass plates [for the negatives]. 6. Collodion. 7. Nitrate of silver bath. 8. Developing solution. 9. Hyposulphate solution. 10. A table made to fold. 11. Legs for the table. 12. Gutta Percha holders. 13. Dish for nitrate bath. 14. Hypo bath. 15. A can for water.
>
> To carry these articles over mountains required good arrangements, but I managed to get them all packed onto a horse, and never met with a single accident.... The disappointments I met with were endless, and certainly prove that a Highland photographer requires patience and perseverance. Often having gone a distance of miles to take some view which I had previously selected, and having started with a brilliant sun and every prospect favourable, the day has overcast just as I got to my ground, rain has come on, or the hills have become obscured by mist, and I had just to wend my way back again. Another enemy that I had to encounter was the most provoking of all, for he appeared on the field very often when the light and everything else was favourable. This enemy was Aeolus the God of Wind. Often did he blow open my tent at the most critical moment of sensitizing a collodion plate, and when he spared the tent, he shook the camera and generally spoiled the picture.[5]

Ross's dark tent can be seen in cat. 51 in this exhibition. The collodion he refers to is a noxious, potentially explosive mixture of gun-cotton and ether. This had to be coated onto the plate in the dark, loaded into the camera, the camera then taken out to the tripod, and the plate developed as soon as the picture was made. I doubt after erecting the tent that one could make pictures at more than two different locations in a single day. Thus the particularly empty scenes by Ross, for instance the rough field of stones depicted in cat. 37, take on a new seriousness. Though even without this context, we may identify this picture with the kind of austere imagery that David Cox was making at Bettws-y-Coed in 1846 for instance (*View near Bettws-y-Coed*, Birmingham Museums and Art Gallery, 32'08).

The shifts that Ross made between the different processes he used, though seeming to belong properly to a technical history, can in fact direct our understanding of his aesthetic orientation. The daguerreotypes now at the Victoria and Albert

Museum are very rare British examples of this difficult process being used outside the professional studio. It is indeed nearly unknown for the amateur, as Ross does, to use the process in outdoor scenes. To my knowledge daguerreotypes were almost wholly confined, within the United Kingdom, to studio portraiture, as the various technical manipulations required demanded highly controlled conditions. In two of these daguerreotypes (cat. 2 and 3) we see his sons fishing on the banks of a river and in the third (cat. 4) a woman (possibly Mrs. Ross, who is known to have hunted deer) shooting a stag. Ross's views on portraiture seem to have been that its aesthetic potential was limited to that of the memento, the highest genre being landscape:

> In my opinion the proper field for the amateur's labour is in the open air...in saying this I am very far from implying that the amateur should never take a portrait, for I must plead guilty to having done so to a considerable extent myself. One of the greatest pleasures I have derived from photography is in having been able to take and retain beside me the likenesses of those most near and dear to me, from the days when they were little children to the hour when they were about to leave their homes for distant lands.[6]

In line with the general drift of romantic naturalism, as exemplified in the secession of the watercolorists from the Royal Academy and their foundation of what in essence was a landscape academy in 1804, the implication appears to be that landscape is the most noble genre that an ambitious photographic artist could aspire to. If this is the case, then nevertheless, while still confined to the small compass of the three-inch daguerreotype, Ross has made a remarkable group of full-length portraits in the setting of the Highland landscape. If one is looking for a pictorial equivalent, then the 1854 full-length portrait of John Ruskin by John Everett Millais comes easily to mind—a similarity of effort that transcends the wide disparity of scale and technique. Here, surely, is the aesthetic of strict optical naturalism from within which the daguerreotype process could find acceptance within the culture into which it was received in the 1840s. Ruskin was himself an amateur daguerreotypist and made, with the assistance of his valets, John Hobbs and Frederick Crawley, a number of remarkable photographs during his visits to Switzerland and Venice in the late 1840s and early 1850s. Ruskin was, of course, deeply ambivalent about photography, though his objections seem to have hinged on the question of its automatic, mechanical process rather than on its indexical quality—for he was a great admirer of the geological fossil, which also bears an indexical relationship to its original.[7] This relationship was one noticed by contemporaries, and it is particularly eloquently expressed by Elizabeth Barrett in a letter of 1843:

> Think of a man sitting down in the sun and leaving his facsimile in all its full completion of outline and shadow, steadfast on a plate, at the end of a minute and a half! The Mesmeric disembodiment of spirits strikes one as a degree less marvellous.... It is not merely the likeness which is precious in such cases—but the association and the sense of the nearness of the thing involved...the fact of the very shadow of the person lying there fixed for ever![8]

Ross seems to have persevered with the daguerreotype until at least 1850, when the last of the portraits at the Victoria and Albert Museum was made. During the late 1840s, as we have seen, he began trials with the calotype process. Unless there is a large volume of unknown early images, this must have proceeded at a fairly sedate pace until the late 1850s when, coinciding with the wave of interest that produced the Photographic Society of Scotland, he produced the bulk of his extant work. The calotype offered a number of advantages over the daguerreotype. For one thing, it was simpler and more predictable, offering, perhaps, the luxury of time to reflect on pictorial rather than technical issues. This was certainly the impression given by the reviewer of the Scottish society's exhibition in 1858: "At first experimenters were too much occupied in working out the problems the art involved to pay much attention to artistic feeling or arrangement; but now we have true art, elegance, grace, and ease united to correct...and beautiful manipulation."[9] Crucial for the attainment of a place within the fine arts, however, was the increase in scale that was possible with the calotype—and clearly as a paper medium its scale relationship to its sister arts of watercolor and printmaking was important if photography was to be accepted as a vehicle for serious artistic production. It is interesting to note that there is indeed a rough parity between the norm of landscape watercolor dimensions and Ross's largest plate size. Certainly these sizes were equivalent to that of small rather than grand exhibition watercolors, but landscape images at this scale were perfectly acceptable as exhibition pieces—particularly as sketches, which, indeed, were part of the theoretical framework within which photography could be most easily assimilated. It is possible that the daguerreotype, being so much smaller, was effectively disqualified from consideration as anything more than a curio in this same arena.

That Ross abandoned the daguerreotype may, I believe, be due largely to his growing aesthetic ambition. In his 1850s calotype work we can discern pictorial concerns that go well beyond the stated aims of his early daguerreian portraiture, and we can detect also a decided shift towards pure landscape and game pictures. As I have said, Ross's education is uncertain. But given his stint in the army we can be fairly sure that he did not go to university and indeed fell well short of the academic training enjoyed by the other gentlemen amateurs practicing photography—men such as Fox Talbot himself, who was a polymath by any standards, and also John Dillwyn Llewelyn, chemist, botanist, and astronomer.[10] We can be certain, however, on the evidence of the photographs themselves, that Ross was visually sophisticated and highly aware of the aesthetic environment of the landscape painting of his day. Indeed, I think his awareness surpasses that of Fox Talbot and Llewelyn and approaches that of Roger Fenton and Benjamin Brecknell Turner.

In the notes he wrote in the 1857 paper, he states that he was using what he terms the "Dr. Diamond method," which was basically a procedural refinement of the Talbot calotype process. We also learn that as an alternative he very rarely used the waxed paper process (which was also basically the calotype technique). Importantly, I think we can trace, in the pictorial negotiations that he struggled with in these processes, an interesting clue to his aesthetic thinking at this date. He found the calotype "wanting in accuracy.... the fault that I found was [that] the hills when beyond the distance of a mile or two, were perfectly flat [having] the appearance of a map or piece of paste board." He thus abandoned paper for glass and took up the collodion process described in his account of his photographic excursions. But, crucially, he returned to the paper process again a short time afterwards. Certainly by 1859 the reviewer of the Edinburgh exhibition is lamenting this return, saying that in his view Ross's calotypes were "not quite up to the mark" and that he should return to the collodion that he had exclusively used previously.[11] Why this about-turn occurred has to do with his deep involvement with the iconography of the Picturesque. Clearly, his subjects fall squarely within the central imagery of that aesthetic. We find the same high-shouldered hillsides that we discover in the iconography of Thomas Hearne, Thomas Girtin, and Paul Sandby Munn (cat. 40), and we find the horizon line pushed up into the uppermost margins of the sheet (cat. 33). This formal strategy produces a classic Picturesque emphasis on the foreground. We also find a marked interest in the cottage (cat. 29) and a general understanding of the value of "broken tints" and that essential quality of Picturesqueness—the rough textures of crumbling stone. Additionally, the device of a screening foreground of trees through which the view is made appears conspicuously as a feature in much of the work (cat. 8). But I think we can identify, in his allegiance to the paper negative, an understanding that a full and appropriate Picturesque response would depend on the graphic means of the construction of the image matching the main subject interests of the Picturesque aesthetic—that is, a general roughness of texture. In this he is recognizing the exact graphic problems that led Cox to turn to the rough flecked wrapping paper that later became associated with his name as "Cox Paper." The paper calotype negative produces a much softer, granulated, diffuse effect in its rendering of the image than does the much sharper collodion. As the calotype image forms in the depths of the paper negative rather than on the surface, as it does in the glass process, the image is already diffuse; and, in printing through the fibers of this negative, rather more diffusion takes place. Collodion had been invented in 1848 and, in terms of its high definition, had technically superseded the paper process by the time it was announced in 1851. Certainly, I think, by 1858 the survival of the paper negative can be attributed, in the hands of aesthetically sophisticated amateurs such as B. B. Turner[12] and Ross himself, to an understanding that the decorum and internal cohesion of Picturesque aesthetics demanded a suitable photo*graphic* equivalent.

In this respect, it is interesting to note that in the contemporary debate over the artistic possibilities of photography there were those who regarded sharp focus as a detrimental quality. Sir William Newton, for example, recommended throwing the image out of focus in order to obtain a more aesthetic effect. Such a preference may be seen to reflect three related theoretical stances already in force in painting: firstly, that such defocusing would produce "breadth" (that is, the photograph's natural detail would be reduced to broad areas of chiaroscuro); secondly, that this same process would produce an "ideal" image—one removed from the contingencies of the imperfect phenomenal world; and, thirdly, that the intervention of the photographer, in defocusing the image, would fulfill the demand for the intervention of the sensibility that was felt, by some, to be lacking in the automatic photographic mechanism.[13]

It is possible to detect in the theoretical base to the Picturesque certain features that underpin the rise of photography. In essence, the choice of screens of trees and hillsides and the new concentration of foreground detail evident in the Picturesque can be seen as the natural corollary of a turning away from the prospect view. What lies beneath this preference is the same deep strata of anti-rationalism that underlies so many of the various intellectual phenomena associated after 1750 with the rise of Romanticism and which may be seen to underlie the invention of photography itself. After this date we observe an increased tendency to divide mental faculties into reason and emotion, intellect and sensation, in which emotion and sensation are accorded supremacy. The Picturesque is an aesthetic of the tactile over the visual—the senses over the intellect (identified here, of course, with sight). Thus, in the enjoyment of the foreground over the distance, and of decayed stone and rough bark, or broken tints and variegated chiaroscuro, we have a preference profoundly in keeping with the deepest psychological needs of the time. This anti-rationalism and its corresponding preference for instinct give rise to a variety of late eighteenth- and early nineteenth-century intellectual phenomena. It underpins, for example, the cult of the primitive, of the child, and even of the mad, and it gives rise, indeed, to the cult of nature itself and thus the prominence accorded to landscape imagery at this time. In the preference for the natural over the artificial (or cultural), we have a preference also for the instinctive and emotive faculties over self-conscious reason. It is on account of this that a sketch aesthetic grew in the late eighteenth century and rose to its height in the 1820s and 1830s with the brilliant virtuoso performances of Bonington and Cox. (Indeed, the purchase of a Cox was sometimes taken to include the experience of its making—patrons paying to be present during the blaze of activity in the creation of the piece. In Bonington's case we have a similar appropriateness in his historical imagery of the seventeenth century, where one senses in his troubadour pieces that his courtiers would be capable of a spontaneous swordsmanship to match the supple wrist of the artist himself.)[14]

The ideal of such pictures is the eye-to-hand virtuosity that in some senses bypasses the rational faculties, and it is in this context that we must see photography. The absence of the conscious interpreter that is prized above all in these works of "natural genius" also translates into photography—the lens replacing the eye and the sensitive emulsion substituted for the hand. Of course, this view is unfashionable today on two counts. In the context of recent deconstructive analysis, the supposed value-free status of the photographic image is under attack. We must remember, though, that such a view when projected into history without care is anachronistic. Certainly, in the context of painting, at photography's birth the new medium would have seemed relatively free of the interventions of the maker. The most this objection can do is to remind us that such ideas of spontaneity must only involve the *fantasy* of the absence of human consciousness. Another objection may arise in that traditional pre-photographic history is usually framed in the form both of a gradual coming into consciousness of the delimiting edge as a conscious decision and, perhaps more importantly, of the gradual adoption of the cone of vision as the ultimate standard of naturalism—one which indicates a new emphasis on the individual observer.[15] In this account, however, the cult of the irrational is generally ignored. This is precisely the opposite of the actual intellectual orientation of the day. And, in fact, just the opposite case is to be found within the Picturesque: here the cone of vision inherent to the prospect view is denied and perspective minimized by curtains of foreground imagery. The effect is thus to lessen the sense of the observing individual as a consciousness literally "above" nature.

I think we can see Ross's deerstalking in the context of this argument. For the ideal stalker is a man of instinct embedded within nature. The most prized quality of the hunter is not the intellect but a sort of cunning, which is a type almost of animal instinct. And clearly the hunter engaged in a grouse or waterfowl shoot is celebrated for his reactions—his spontaneous ability to shoot without thinking. In fact, Ross was praised for this gift by C. H. Wheeler in his book *Sportascrapiana* of 1867: "Captain Ross was noted from his youth as a genuine specimen of the innate deer stalker, unsurpassed with the rifle." It may be interesting to note that at least one observer has remarked that Ross's deerstalking skills of "undetected advancement" have informed his approach to photographic composition through a screen of trees. If this is indeed the case, then Ross may be seen as a prime example of Jay Appleton's prospect-refuge theory. Professor Appleton is a geographer interested in the psychology of the human habitat as evidenced in the fine arts. He sees such subjects as conditioned by our ancient need to see and not be seen. This may indeed be the case, but it is difficult to sustain the theory over a wider period of landscape art and also into more diverse pictorial forms. As I have outlined, it seems more likely that Ross's devices are conditioned by the aesthetic norms of the high Picturesque.[16]

During our time, when some photographic artists have abandoned even the camera as too predatory an instrument, it is difficult to see Ross's game pictures in the correct perspective.[17] So profoundly out of key with our modern sensibilities are these pictures that we might tend to minimize their importance in Ross's oeuvre. If we are to understand the most basic strata of his intellectual orientation, however, I believe these pictures must be faced.

Any modern assessment is clearly problematic, for our own stance on their content is alien to say the least—informed as it is likely to be by the modern cult of wilderness nature and the emotional ambience of the conservation movement. For Ross, however, it is evident that his sport was natural—a logical and intrinsic part of his fundamental mind-set towards nature and man's place within the world-scheme (I might almost say "Creation"). For us his hunting activities perhaps speak of a dominion over nature that few within the arts would claim any right to today, and this may seem at odds with the emotional and intellectual orientation of his thinking as implied by his aesthetic. In the terms of his own time such a view is untenable. For if one approaches his basic Romanticism from within—bearing in mind that the whole effort of the romantic ideal was to integrate man with nature—then it must be conceded that the greatest sign of that integration should be a comfort with one's actions in the world. It may not be too wide of the mark to think of him conceiving of his hunting as part of nature. As ever, though, our interpretations of history reveal as much about our own anxieties and hopes as the subject of our study.

Notes

1 Cornelius Varley (1781–1873) was a watercolorist who invented the Patent Graphic Telescope, a drawing aid based on the camera lucida. He won medals for his scientific instruments at the Great Exhibition of 1851. For a discussion of his interest in optical phenomena, see my essay "Der englische romantische Naturalismus de Kreis um Cornelius Varley" in *Englische Aquarelle der Romantik,* Staatliche Museen zu Berlin, Nationalgalerie, 1990, pp. 21-24.

2 For the Delamottes, see Alec Stirling, "Philip Henry Delamotte: Artist and Photographer," *Royal Society of Arts Journal,* CXXXVIII, no. 5407, June 1990, pp. 491-95.

3 For the Landseer portraits, see Sotheby's, 24 June 1971, lot 31; Christie's, 18 November 1983, lot 1; and Parke-Bernet, New York, 14 May 1976, lot 63. The daguerreotype is in the Victoria and Albert Museum, London; Mrs. Ross's photograph is in the Getty Museum, Malibu, California; Fenton's portraits are in the Royal Library at Windsor. Several copies of other photographic and printed portraits are in the Ross file in the Photographs Section in the Collection of Prints, Drawings and Paintings at the V&A.

4 C. A. Wheeler, *Sportascrapiana,* London, 1867, p. 110.

5 *Photographic Notes,* March 15, 1857, pp. 95-97.

6 Ibid.

7 For a discussion of the indexical nature of the photograph, see my introduction to *The Tree,* exhibition catalogue, Usher Art Gallery, Lincoln, 1987, pp. 6-15.

8 Quoted in Mark Haworth-Booth, ed., *The Golden Age of British Photography,* V&A and Aperture, 1984, p. 25.

9 *The Daily Scotsman,* December 18, 1858. This and other press clippings relating to the Photographic Society of Scotland can be seen at the Scottish Record Office, Edinburgh (ref. GD356/4).

10 See Mike Weaver, "Fox Talbot: Conversation Pieces" and my essay, "Llewelyn: Instantaneity and Transience," both in *British Photography in the Nineteenth Century: The Fine Art Tradition,* ed. Weaver, Cambridge University Press, New York, 1989.

11 *The Photographic Journal,* January 15, 1859, p. 23.

12 For Turner, see Mark Haworth-Booth, "Benjamin Brecknell Turner: Photographic Views from Nature," also in Weaver, ed. (see note 10).

13 For Newton, see Beaumont Newhall, ed., *Photography: Essays and Images,* Museum of Modern Art, New York, 1980, and Carolyn Bloore and Grace Seiberling, *A Vision Exchanged,* V&A, 1985.

14 For Cox, see *David Cox,* Birmingham Museum and Art Gallery, 1983, cat. 123; for Bonington, see Patrick Noon, *Richard Parkes Bonington: "On the Pleasure of Painting,"* Yale Center for British Art, New Haven, 1991.

15 See, for example, Peter Galassi, *Before Photography,* Museum of Modern Art, New York, 1981, especially pages 16-17.

16 Jay Appleton, *The Experience of Landscape,* University of Hull, 1975. Ross's deerstalking skills are referred to in the catalogue to the exhibition, *The Waking Dream,* ed. Maria Morris Hambourg and Pierre Apraxine, Metropolitan Museum of Art, New York, 1993, p. 374.

17 For the camera as predator, see *The Tree* (see note 7).

Sources

Photographs by Ross are in the collections of the following museums: The Victoria and Albert Museum, London; The J. Paul Getty Museum, Malibu, California; The Metropolitan Museum of Art, New York; The Science Museum, London.

Several albums of Ross photographs are known: The present works come from the album in the possession of Janet Lehr, Inc., New York. (The album is fully illustrated in her catalogue, vol. 7, numbers 3 and 4, 1986.) Another is in the possession of Hans Kraus, Fine Photographs, New York. Kraus has also sold a third album to a private collector. A number of these are illustrated in his catalogue, *Sun Pictures,* volume one, New York, nd.

Ross correspondence can be found in the Scottish Record Office (ref. GD356/1-20) and the National Library of Scotland, Edinburgh (refs. MS. 15188, 15189, 15048, 4411, 15197, 23221, 23222, and a copy of Ross's speech at a political meeting in 1832). Sara Stevenson and Alison Morrison-Low's *Scottish Photography, A Bibliography,* Edinburgh, 1990, gives references to Ross's own writings and reviews mentioning his work in the various photographic journals. His obituaries are on file in the Photographs Section at the V&A.

Glossary

An **albumen print** is a photograph in which the paper has first been glazed with egg whites before being sensitized to light with a silver nitrate solution. The image thus forms on the surface rather than in the depth of the paper. The process was invented by L. D. Blanquart-Evrard in 1850.

The **calotype** is an improved version of Fox Talbot's photogenic drawing process of about 1835. He patented the improved method in 1841. Writing paper is coated with a solution of silver nitrate and various other chemicals, exposed in the camera, and then developed to form the negative. Using basically the same chemistry and a piece of writing paper placed in contact with the negative, a print can be made.

The **collodion process** uses glass instead of paper as the negative base. Collodion is made from pyroxyline (an explosive) dissolved in alcohol and ether. This is coated onto glass and made light-sensitive with various salts and silver nitrate. The process was invented by Frederick Scott Archer in 1848 but was only demonstrated publicly in 1851.

A **contact print** is produced by placing a negative over a piece of sensitized writing paper. These are held together in a glazed wooden frame and exposed to sunlight. The print is thus the exact same size as the negative.

The **daguerreotype** uses a polished silver-coated sheet of copper. The silver is made light-sensitive with iodine fumes. The exposed image is later developed using mercury vapor. The process was invented in the mid-1830s but only announced in 1839.

For further details see Brian Coe and Mark Haworth-Booth, *A Guide to Early Photographic Processes*, Victoria and Albert Museum, London, 1983.

cat. 8 *At Aros—Mull*

cat. 20 [Dead Stag on a Sledge]

cat. 26 [Glenforsa House, Isle of Mull]

cat. 29 [Rustic Shed by a Road]

cat. 37 [Rocky Hillside]

cat. 38 [Shepherd's Hut]

cat. 40 [A Gorge]

cat. 43 *Banks of the River Affric*

cat. 47 [Rocky Coastline]

cat. 51 [Rocky Landscape with Ross's Dark Tent]

Checklist

Items 1 through 7, a group of daguerreotypes in the Victoria and Albert Museum, represent the earliest known photographs by Horatio Ross. Items 8 through 53 come from an album of 110 albumen prints by Horatio Ross assembled for his wife, Justine. The cover of the album is embossed: "Justine H. Ross/1870." The prints are mounted on album pages measuring 14 11/16 x 17 3/4 in (356 x 452 mm). The order of the photographs in this exhibition does not follow the sequence in the album. For reproductions of all 110 photographs with indications of their original order in the album, see *Horatio Ross Presentation Album: Justine H. Ross, 1870* (Janet Lehr, Inc., vol. 7, nos. 3 and 4, March 1986). Only a few of the photographs are labeled; the titles within brackets have been supplied for this exhibition. Unless otherwise noted, all exhibited photographs from the album are in the possession of Janet Lehr, New York.

1 [Self-Portrait], c. 1850
Daguerreotype
3 3/4 x 2 3/4 in (95 x 70 mm)
The Board of Trustees of the
Victoria and Albert Museum, London

2 *Hoddy* [Horatio Ross, Jr.] *and John Monro Fishing at Flaipool,* 1847
Daguerreotype
2 11/16 x 3 11/16 in (69 x 94 mm)
Inscribed in pencil on paper backing:
Hoddy and John Monro fishing at Flaipool/1847
The Board of Trustees of the
Victoria and Albert Museum, London

3 *Horatio and Colin Ross and Old David Dear Fishing at the Falls of Rossie,* 1848
Daguerreotype
3 3/16 x 2 5/8 in (82 x 68 mm)
Inscribed in pencil on paper backing:
Horatio and Colin Ross and Old David Dear fishing at the falls of Rossie/April 1848/no. 37
The Board of Trustees of the
Victoria and Albert Museum, London

4 *Craigdarcort,* 1848
Daguerreotype
3 3/16 x 2 11/16 in (82 x 69 mm)
Inscribed in pencil on paper backing:
Craigdarcort/no. 24/1848
The Board of Trustees of the
Victoria and Albert Museum, London

5 [Portrait of a Lady], c. 1850
Daguerreotype
3 3/4 x 2 3/4 in (95 x 70 mm)
The Board of Trustees of the
Victoria and Albert Museum, London

6 *Hercules Ross at Balfour*, 1850
Daguerreotype
2 1/4 x 1 13/16 in (58 x 46 mm)
Inscribed in pencil on paper backing:
Hercules Ross at Balfour/January 1850/
no. 67
The Board of Trustees of the
Victoria and Albert Museum, London

7 [Edward Ross], c. 1850
Daguerreotype
5 1/8 x 4 1/8 in (130 x 105 mm)
The Board of Trustees of the
Victoria and Albert Museum, London

8 *At Aros—Mull*, 1866
Albumen print from glass negative
9 11/16 x 12 1/8 in (246 x 308 mm)
Inscribed in pencil on mount:
Aros–Mull–April 1866–collodion
Herbert Davis Cooperman

9 [Dunottar Castle, Kincardineshire],
c. 1858
Albumen print from paper negative
8 13/16 x 12 15/16 in (223 x 329 mm)
Magnum Opus

10 *St. Mary's, Cowie* [Stirlingshire], c. 1858
Albumen print from paper negative
7 1/8 x 12 3/16 in (181 x 310 mm)
Inscribed in pencil on mount:
St. Mary's, Cowie!

11 *Wyis Lodge* [Wyvis Lodge, Ross],
c. 1866
Albumen print from paper negative
7 7/8 x 12 7/8 in (200 x 327 mm)
Inscribed in pencil on mount:
Wyis Lodge

12 [Landscape with a Fence], c. 1858
Albumen print from paper negative
8 3/8 x 12 13/16 in (214 x 326 mm)

13 [Farm Buildings], c. 1858
Albumen print from paper negative
7 3/4 x 12 5/8 in (196 x 321 mm)

14 *Glen Dibidal* [Glen Diebidale, Ross],
1859
Albumen print from glass negative
9 x 13 1/16 in (229 x 332 mm)
Inscribed in pencil on mount:
Glen Dibidal–1859/collodion
Herbert Davis Cooperman

15 [Dead Stag on a Cart], before 1858
Albumen print from paper/glass
negative?
10 1/2 x 13 1/4 in (267 x 337 mm)
Inscribed on verso of mount in pencil:
Horatio Ross Edinburgh before 1858
Herbert Davis Cooperman

16 *Weary, So Weary of Living;*
Longing To Lie Down and Die, c. 1858
Albumen print from glass negative
9 1/4 x 12 3/4 in (235 x 324 mm)
Inscribed in pencil on mount:
"Weary, so weary of living;"
longing to lie down & die

17 *Home They Brought the Warrior Dead,* c. 1858
Albumen print from paper/glass negative
$9\frac{7}{8}$ x $13\frac{1}{8}$ in (252 x 333 mm)
Inscribed in pencil on the mount:
"Home they brought the warrior dead"

18 [Dead Stag], c. 1858
Albumen print from glass negative
$10\frac{3}{8}$ x $13\frac{3}{8}$ in (264 x 340 mm)

19 *The Four Graces*, c. 1858
Albumen print from glass negative
$8\frac{3}{4}$ x $13\frac{5}{16}$ in (222 x 338 mm)
Inscribed in pencil on the mount:
The four Graces
Herbert Davis Cooperman

20 [Dead Stag on a Sledge], c. 1858
Albumen print from glass negative
$10\frac{1}{8}$ x $13\frac{3}{8}$ in (257 x 340 mm)
Herbert Davis Cooperman

21 [Grange Road, Edinburgh?], c. 1858
Albumen print from paper negative
$9\frac{3}{8}$ x $13\frac{7}{16}$ in (239 x 342 mm)

22 [Middle Meadow Walk, Edinburgh], c. 1858
Albumen print from paper negative
$9\frac{5}{8}$ x $13\frac{1}{16}$ in (245 x 332 mm)

23 [George Heriot's Hospital, Edinburgh], c. 1858
Albumen print from paper negative
$9\frac{1}{2}$ x $13\frac{1}{8}$ in (242 x 333 mm)

24 [Bonar Bridge, Sutherland], c. 1858
Albumen print from paper negative
$9\frac{11}{16}$ x $13\frac{3}{16}$ in (246 x 335 mm)

25 [Glenforsa House, Isle of Mull], c. 1858
Albumen print from glass negative
$10\frac{3}{8}$ x 12 in (264 x 305 mm)

26 [Glenforsa House, Isle of Mull], c. 1858
Albumen print from glass negative
$10\frac{5}{8}$ x $13\frac{1}{4}$ in (270 x 337 mm)

27 [Wooden Bridge], c. 1858
Albumen print from paper negative
$10\frac{1}{8}$ x $12\frac{15}{16}$ in (257 x 329 mm)

28 [Stone Bridge], c. 1858
Albumen print from paper negative
$10\frac{1}{8}$ x $13\frac{5}{16}$ in (257 x 338 mm)

29 [Rustic Shed by a Road], c. 1858
Albumen print from paper negative
$10\frac{1}{4}$ x $12\frac{5}{8}$ in (261 x 321 mm)

30 [A Woodland Path], c. 1858
Albumen print from glass negative
$9\frac{3}{4}$ x $12\frac{1}{2}$ in (247 x 318 mm)

31 [Waterfall], c. 1858
Albumen print from paper negative
$9\frac{3}{4}$ x $13\frac{1}{4}$ in (247 x 337 mm)

32 [Tree], c. 1858
Albumen print from paper negative
$13\frac{3}{8}$ x $9\frac{3}{4}$ in (340 x 247 mm)

33 [Waterfall], c. 1858
Albumen print from glass negative
$10\frac{7}{16}$ x $12\frac{5}{8}$ in (265 x 321 mm)

34 [Waterfall], c. 1858
Albumen print from paper negative
13 x 10 in (330 x 254 mm)

35 [Trees by a Loch], c. 1858
Albumen print from paper negative
10 x $13\frac{1}{4}$ in (254 x 337 mm)

36 [Boat on a Rocky Shore], c. 1858
Albumen print from paper negative
10 3/8 x 12 13/16 in (264 x 326 mm)

37 [Rocky Hillside], c. 1858
Albumen print from paper negative
10 1/16 x 12 9/16 in (256 x 320 mm)

38 [Shepherd's Hut], 1858
Albumen print from paper negative
9 5/8 x 12 7/8 in (245 x 327 mm)
Inscribed in pencil on mount:
Ross. 1858

39 [Snow Scene], c. 1858
Albumen print from glass negative
10 1/2 x 13 1/4 in (267 x 337 mm)

40 [A Gorge], c. 1858
Albumen print from paper negative
9 7/8 x 12 3/4 in (252 x 324 mm)

41 [River View], c. 1858
Albumen print from paper negative
9 7/8 x 12 1/2 in (252 x 318 mm)

42 [River Gorge], c. 1858
Albumen print from paper negative
9 7/8 x 12 5/16 in (252 x 313 mm)
Magnum Opus

43 *Banks of the River Affric* [Inverness-shire], c. 1858
Albumen print from paper negative
9 1/2 x 12 15/16 in (242 x 329 mm)
Inscribed in pencil on mount:
Banks of river Affaric. 1858/wax paper

44 [A Rocky Headland], c. 1858
Albumen print from paper negative
9 9/16 x 13 1/4 in (243 x 337 mm)
Herbert Davis Cooperman

45 [River Affric?], c. 1858
Albumen print from paper negative
10 3/8 x 12 15/16 in (264 x 329 mm)

46 [Rocky Stream], c. 1858
Albumen print from paper negative
9 5/16 x 12 3/16 in (237 x 310 mm)

47 [Rocky Coastline], c. 1858
Albumen print from glass negative
10 1/8 x 13 1/4 in (257 x 337 mm)

48 [Natural Bridge], c. 1858
Albumen print from glass negative
10 5/8 x 12 9/16 in (270 x 320 mm)

49 [Rocky Landscape], c. 1858
Albumen print from paper negative
10 1/8 x 12 3/4 in (257 x 324 mm)

50 [Rocky Landscape with Ross's Dark Tent], c. 1858
Albumen print from glass negative
9 1/8 x 12 5/16 in (232 x 313 mm)

51 [Rocky Landscape with Ross's Dark Tent], c. 1858
Albumen print from glass negative
10 7/8 x 10 5/16 in (276 x 262 mm)

52 [Scottish Tower House], c. 1858
Albumen print from paper negative
10 1/2 x 13 1/16 in (267 x 332 mm)

53 [Trees by a Loch], c. 1858
Albumen print from glass negative
9 5/8 x 13 3/8 in (245 x 340 mm)